PANCAKE TORTOISE AS PET

COMPLETE OWNERS GUIDE TO PANCAKE TORTOISE BEHAVIOR, HEALTHY TRAINING, DIET, REPRODUCTION AND HAPPY HOME

ALBERT A. NELSON

CONTENTS

INTRODUCTION..**5**

CHAPTER 1 ....**9**

CHOOSING A PANCAKE TORTOISE.................................9

CHAPTER 2 ....**16**

CREATING THE IDEAL ENVIRONMENT 16

CHAPTER 3 ....**23**

FEEDING AND NUTRITION...23

CHAPTER 4 ....**31**

MEDICAL AND VETERINARY CARE 31

CHAPTER 5 ....**40**

SOCIALIZATION AND HANDLING...................................40

CHAPTER 6 ....**49**

REPRODUCTION AND BREEDING 49

CHAPTER 7 ....**56**

LEGAL CONCERNS 56

CHAPTER 8 ....**65**

TROUBLESHOOTING MANUAL 65

BONUS CHAPTER..**76**

FAQS 76

INTRODUCTION

Reptile fans possess a distinct interest for people looking for unique and engaging companions. The Pancake Tortoise (Malacochersus tornieri) distinguishes out among these remarkable critters due to its unusual flat, pancake-like shell. This part provides an introduction to the complex world of caring for these unique reptiles, diving into their quirks and highlighting the critical significance of giving them with attentive and adequate care.

AN INTRODUCTION TO PANCAKE TORTOISES

Pancake tortoises are members of the Testudinidae family and are native to East Africa's desert regions. Their scientific name, Malacochersus tornieri, emphasizes their distinct physical characteristics as well as their position within the tortoise family. Pancake tortoises, unlike their domed relatives, have an unusually flat and flexible shell that allows them to navigate the rocky fissures of their natural habitat with incredible agility.

A Pancake Tortoise's carapace is not only a remarkable adaptation for survival, but also a distinguishing trait that captivates reptile fans. Its flattened look is an evolutionary reaction to their habitat, allowing them to squeeze into small gaps and avoid predators.

Understanding the natural behavior and habits of Pancake Tortoises, in addition to their physical qualities, is critical for providing best care. These tortoises are primarily herbivores, eating a variety of grasses, leaves, and occasionally fruits. Their semi-arboreal nature further distinguishes them, since they are frequently observed in their native habitat climbing rocks or low plants.

THE IMPORTANCE OF CARE

It is our responsibility as caretakers of these unique creatures to understand the need of giving correct care for Pancake Tortoises. The obligations go beyond simply providing food and shelter; they also include developing an atmosphere that resembles their natural habitat and caring to their individual needs.

Proper care is not just a moral imperative, but also a requirement for the well-being and lifespan of captive Pancake Tortoises. Caretakers can replicate situations that promote physical and psychological well-being by understanding their food needs, environmental preferences, and social behaviors.

The complexities of their care extend beyond surface-level considerations. Pancake tortoises require considerable attention to detail because to their particular diet and habitat requirements. Inadequate care can result in a variety of health problems, such as metabolic abnormalities and shell malformations. As a result, this part acts as a wake-up call to wannabe caregivers, emphasizing the positive impact of responsible ownership on the general health and happiness of these wonderful reptiles.

CHAPTER 1

CHOOSING A PANCAKE TORTOISE

The process of bringing a Pancake Tortoise into your life is a serious commitment that requires careful consideration and research. In this chapter, we begin the process of picking a Pancake Tortoise, delving into the delicate aspects of selecting a healthy companion and acquiring a full understanding of the species' distinctive qualities.

SELECTING A HEALTHY TORTOISE

Choosing a Pancake Tortoise is a critical decision that takes careful inspection, a keen eye, and knowledge of the signs of a healthy animal. Certain characteristics should guide your decision process whether you buy from a breeder, a reputable reptile store, or a rescue organization.

1.PHYSICAL APPEARANCE: Examine the tortoise's overall physical condition first. A healthy Pancake Tortoise should have clear eyes that are free of discharge or puffiness. The nostrils should be clear, and there should be no symptoms of infection or redness in the mouth. The shell, which is a distinguishing trait of these tortoises, should be hard with no soft patches or abnormalities. Any irregularities in these areas could indicate underlying health difficulties.

2.ACTIVE BEHAVIOR: A tortoise in good health has a lively and alert demeanor. An active tortoise will be curious and will explore its surroundings with purpose. While some tortoises may first retreat into their shells when approached, a healthy species should be eager to interact with its surroundings.

3.APPETITE AND FEEDING HABITS: It is critical to assess the tortoise's appetite and feeding habits. A healthy Pancake Tortoise should be interested in food and have a diverse and robust appetite. Keep an eye on its eating habits and make sure it eats a well-balanced diet. A lack of interest in food or inconsistent eating patterns may be warning flags that should be investigated further.

4. Respiratory Health: Watch the tortoise's breathing habits. Respiration that is labored or wheezing may suggest a respiratory problem. A healthy tortoise should be able to breathe steadily and quietly. Ascertain that the ambient temperature is appropriate, as incorrect temperatures might contribute to respiratory difficulties.

5. Limbs and Tail Examine the limbs and tail for any symptoms of damage, swelling, or abnormalities. The limbs should be able to move, and the tail should be free

of deformities. Any signs of lameness or difficulty moving should be evaluated by a veterinarian.

Remember that the choosing procedure is about assuring the well-being of the creature you put into your care, not just getting a visually stunning tortoise. A thorough examination, together with knowledge of the species' habits, establishes the groundwork for a pleasurable and responsible reptile ownership experience.

SPECIES CHARACTERISTICS UNDERSTANDING

Each tortoise species has distinct characteristics and habits that influence how it interacts with its surroundings. To fully care for a Pancake Tortoise, one must delve into the complexities of its species traits, unraveling the fabric of its natural impulses and adaptations.

1. Semi-Arboreal Nature: One of the most distinguishing characteristics of Pancake Tortoises is their semi-arboreal nature. Unlike many other tortoise species that prefer to stay on the ground, Pancake Tortoises enjoy climbing. Their flattened shells allow them to move easily in rough terrain, allowing them to ascend low vegetation or seek refuge in elevated spots. Consider vertical aspects that cater to this specific activity, such as possibilities for climbing and exploring, when designing an enclosure.

2. Food Preferences: Pancakes Tortoises are herbivores who like a diversified, high-fiber diet. They graze on grasses, leaves, and occasionally fruits in their natural habitat. In captivity, emulating this diet is critical for their nutritional well-being. Maintain a calcium-rich diet to promote shell growth and overall health. A well-researched and balanced diet contributes greatly to the vigor and longevity of the tortoise.

3.   Temperature   and   Lighting   Requirements: Understanding Pancake Tortoises' thermal needs is critical for designing a setting that resembles their natural surroundings. These tortoises require a basking area with temperatures ranging from 90-95°F (32-35°C) and a colder area with temperatures ranging from 75-80°F (24-27°C). Furthermore, access to natural sunshine or UVB lighting is required for the creation of vitamin D3, which is required for calcium metabolism and shell health.

4. Social Behavior: Pancake Tortoises have social habits and are known to tolerate the presence of conspecifics better than many other tortoise species. However, it is critical to keep an eye on interactions to avoid aggressiveness or tension. When housing numerous tortoises, make sure the cage is sufficiently enough and has hiding spaces to prevent territorial disputes.

5. Hibernation Considerations: During the dry season, Pancake Tortoises go into a state of aestivation, which is similar to hibernation. While captive tortoises may not hibernate completely, giving a colder phase with less light can simulate this natural cycle. However, approaching hibernation with caution is essential, since inappropriate conditions might lead to health concerns.

Caretakers can modify their approach to fit the special demands of Pancake Tortoises by understanding these species-specific traits. This understanding is the foundation for establishing a setting that not only supports the tortoise's physical health but also allows it to display natural behaviors, ensuring a pleasant and enriching existence in captivity.

CHAPTER 2

Creating the Ideal Environment

Providing an appropriate environment for Pancake Tortoises is a difficult task that involves diligent planning and a thorough understanding of the species' natural behaviors. In this chapter, we will look at the important components of creating an environment that mimics the conditions of their natural habitat, supporting their well-being, and laying the groundwork for a thriving life in captivity.

SETUP OF THE ENCLOSURE

1. Size and Dimensions: The enclosure's size is crucial in guaranteeing the comfort and health of Pancake Tortoises. Because of their semi-arboreal nature and energetic behaviors, a large enclosure is required. A minimum enclosure size of 4 feet by 8 feet is

recommended for a single adult tortoise to allow for movement and exploration. Increase the size of the enclosure if you have numerous tortoises to avoid territorial disputes.

2. Enclosure and Fencing Material: Build the enclosure with materials that provide both security and ventilation. Choose strong walls to keep out drafts and protect the tortoises from predators. A combination of solid walls and mesh roofing or sides can provide appropriate airflow while preserving a secure atmosphere.

3. Climbing Structures: Because Pancake Tortoises are semi-arboreal, integrate climbing structures throughout the cage. They can display their natural behavior by using rocks, branches, or purpose-built platforms. To avoid accidents or injuries, ensure that these constructions are stable and securely placed.

4. Secure outside Access: Provide secure outside access to natural sunlight if possible. UVB exposure in outdoor enclosures aids in the synthesis of vitamin D3, which is required for calcium metabolism. Make sure the outside space is escape-proof and has shady areas to prevent overheating.

5. Tortoise Subdivision: When housing numerous Pancake Tortoises, consider forming subdivisions within the enclosure. This allows for geographical divisions and reduces the likelihood of conflict. To avoid resource rivalry, each subdivision should have its own feeding and bathing areas.

REQUIREMENTS FOR TEMPERATURE AND LIGHTING

1. Basking space: Establish a designated basking space with temperatures ranging from 90 to 95 degrees Fahrenheit (32 to 35 degrees Celsius). To achieve and maintain this temperature, use heat lamps or ceramic

heat emitters. Make sure the basking space is easily accessible and spacious enough for the tortoises to absorb heat comfortably.

2. Cooler Zones: Create cooler zones within the enclosure with temperatures ranging from 75 to 80°F (24 to 27°C). The tortoises can so alter their body temperature as needed. To generate a heat gradient within the enclosure, place these places distant from the basking spot.

3. Nighttime Temperature decline: Allow a steady decline in temperature during the night to mimic natural temperature swings. The tortoises' normal circadian rhythms are supported by this nocturnal chill, which is typically roughly 10°F (5-6°C) lower than the daylight temperature.

4. UVB Lighting: Provide UVB lighting to ensure vitamin D3 production. UVB is essential for calcium absorption and shell health. Use reptile-safe UVB lamps and make sure the tortoises have access to this lighting for 10-12 hours per day.

DECOR AND SUBSTRATE

1. Substrate Choice:

Select a substrate that closely resembles the natural environment of Pancake Tortoises. An appropriate substrate is made up of topsoil, coconut coir, and cypress mulch. Avoid substrates that may be hazardous to swallowing, such as coarse sands or loose particles.

2. Natural Decor: Add natural decor items to the enclosure. Rocks, logs, and plants form a visually fascinating habitat that invites investigation. Make sure the decor is safe and devoid of any hazards that could hurt the tortoises.

3. food Plants: Incorporate food plants into the enclosure to increase grazing opportunities. Ensure that the plants you choose are pesticide-free and safe to eat. Edible flora not only gives nutritional variety but also helps the tortoises with their natural foraging activity.

ENRICHMENT AND HIDING SPOTS

1. Hiding Places and Shelters:

Include shelters and hiding places within the enclosure to meet the tortoises' security needs. Half-logs, purpose-built shelters, or rock formations serve as refuges for tortoises to rest or flee perceived predators. Make sure hiding places are easily available and evenly scattered within the enclosure.

2. Enrichment Activities: Provide diverse activities that stimulate the tortoises' natural behaviors in their environment. To promote foraging, scatter food items about the enclosure. To engage their senses, place

unique objects such as tortoise-safe toys or items with varied textures. Enrichment encourages physical activity and mental stimulation, which improves their general well-being.

3. Interaction and Socialization: If you have several Pancake Tortoises, pay attention to their interactions and social dynamics. Although Pancake Tortoises are generally tolerant of their conspecifics, keep an eye out for any symptoms of violence or discomfort. Providing multiple feeding and basking locations reduces competition and promotes peaceful coexistence.

CHAPTER 3

Feeding and nutrition

Proper nourishment is essential for the health and lifespan of Pancake Tortoises. In this chapter, we'll look at how to create a well-balanced food, set up a feeding schedule, and grasp the importance of calcium and vitamin supplements in satisfying the dietary needs of these amazing reptiles.

ADEQUATE DIET COMPOSITION

1. Diet of Herbivores:

Pancake tortoises are herbivores who eat grasses, leaves, and even fruits in their natural habitat. In captivity, emulating this herbivorous diet is critical for their nutritional well-being. Leafy greens like dandelion, collard, and mustard greens should be the backbone of their diet.

2. Vegetable Variety:

To promote nutritional variety, include a wide variety of veggies. Consume veggies such as kale, spinach, and broccoli in moderation. However, avoid high-oxalate veggies since oxalates might interfere with calcium absorption.

3. Fruit Consumption is Limited:

While fruits can be served on occasion, they should be consumed in moderation due to their high sugar content. Berries, melons, and papaya are all safe fruit selections. Remove any uneaten fruits as soon as possible to avoid spoiling.

4. High-Protein Food Avoidance:

A low-protein diet is ideal for Pancake Tortoises. Avoid high-protein feeds like commercial tortoise pellets and excessive legume consumption, as these might cause metabolic imbalances and kidney problems.

5. Foods Rich in Calcium:

Calcium is essential for shell growth as well as overall health. Calcium-fortified tortoise pellets, cuttlebone, or powdered calcium supplements are examples of calcium-rich diets. The addition of calcium powder to veggies ensures that tortoises get enough calcium.

6. Food-Based Hydration:

Pancake tortoises get a large percentage of their hydration from the food they eat. To ensure optimum hydration, incorporate moisture-rich veggies in the diet. It is also necessary to provide a shallow water dish for drinking.

7. Seasonal Changes:

When possible, mimic seasonal fluctuations in your diet. Pancake Tortoises in the wild are subject to fluctuations in vegetation availability. Seasonal diet changes can help to provide a more diversified and enriching feeding experience.

FEEDING TIMELINE

1. Routine of Daily Feeding:

Establish a consistent daily feeding regimen for Pancake Tortoises to provide structure and consistency. Every day, provide fresh vegetables and greens to ensure that their diet is well-balanced and meets their nutritional needs.

2. Appetite Control:

Keep a watchful eye on the tortoises' appetites. While some people have voracious appetites, others may be more choosy. Changes in eating patterns might be an indication of a health problem, therefore any substantial drop in appetite should be investigated further.

3. Treats should be consumed in moderation:

While occasional pleasures are permitted, moderation is essential. Small amounts of fruit or edible flowers may be included as treats. Excessive treat consumption, on the other hand, might cause dietary imbalances, negatively damaging the tortoise's health.

4. Individual Needs Tailoring:

Recognize that each Pancake Tortoise has different nutritional preferences and demands. Adjust the feeding schedule to account for changes in appetite, ensuring that each tortoise receives appropriate nutrition.

5. Environmental Benefits of Feeding:

By dispersing food items throughout the enclosure, you can incorporate environmental enrichment into the feeding process. This fosters natural foraging activities while also offering mental and physical stimulation.

SUPPLEMENTS FOR CALCIUM AND VITAMINS

1. The significance of calcium:

Calcium is an important part of a Pancake Tortoise's diet, as it is required for the formation and maintenance of a robust and healthy shell. It is critical in captivity to ensure that tortoises receive adequate dietary calcium to avoid complications like as metabolic bone disease.

2. Ratio of calcium to phosphorus:

Take note of the calcium-to-phosphorus ratio in your diet. A good equilibrium is essential for calcium absorption. Foods having an unbalanced ratio, such as high-phosphorus vegetables, should be consumed in moderation.

3. Supplements for calcium:

Calcium supplements are critical in ensuring that Pancake Tortoises get enough of this important nutrient. Calcium can be given in a variety of forms, such as calcium powder, cuttlebone, or crushed eggshell.

Several times per week, dusting veggies with calcium powder helps them achieve their dietary requirements.

4. Synthesis of Vitamin D3:

Vitamin D3 is required for calcium absorption. While natural sunlight is a good source of vitamin D3, captive tortoises must be supplemented, especially if they do not have access to UVB exposure outside. To support vitamin D3 production, UVB lighting intended for reptiles should be administered for 10-12 hours each day.

5. Supplemental Vitamins:

Pancake Tortoises may benefit from vitamin supplements in addition to calcium, especially if their diet is deficient in specific vitamins. Multivitamin supplements for herbivorous reptiles can be given according to the manufacturer's instructions. However, a well-balanced diet should reduce the need for significant supplementation.

6. Consultation with a veterinarian:

Regular veterinary examinations are essential for checking the overall health of Pancake Tortoises and ensuring that their nutritional requirements are satisfied. Consult a reptile veterinarian to customize supplementing depending on the specific needs of each tortoise.

CHAPTER 4

Medical and Veterinary Care

Keeping Pancake Tortoises healthy requires a proactive commitment to health and veterinary care. In this chapter, we'll look at common health conditions that might afflict these unusual reptiles, identify symptoms of sickness, and discuss the necessity of frequent check-ups and preventive actions in keeping them well.

COMMON HEALTH PROBLEMS

1. Infections of the Respiratory Tract:

Pancake tortoises are prone to respiratory illnesses, which are frequently caused by insufficient temperature and humidity levels. Wheezing, labored breathing, and nasal discharge are all symptoms of a respiratory problem. Maintaining proper environmental conditions is critical in preventing respiratory issues.

2. MBD (Metabolic Bone Disease):

Inadequate calcium intake can result in metabolic bone disease, a disorder that affects the development and strength of the tortoise's shell and bones. MBD is characterized by softening of the shell, drowsiness, and difficulties moving. A calcium-rich diet, adequate lighting, and supplements can all assist to prevent this illness.

3. Abnormalities in the Shell:

Shell abnormalities can occur as a result of poor feeding, insufficient UVB exposure, or poor enclosure conditions. Pyramiding (an irregular development pattern of the shell) and shell abnormalities require immediate care. These anomalies can be avoided by providing a proper nutrition, UVB lighting, and a suitable atmosphere.

4. Infections caused by parasites:

Internal and external parasites can cause lethargy, weight loss, and changes in fecal consistency in Pancake Tortoises. A veterinarian's regular fecal checks can diagnose and treat parasite diseases. Preventive methods include keeping the enclosure clean and exercising excellent hygiene.

5. Infections of the eyes and mouth:

Infections of the eyes or mouth can occur, and are frequently the result of poor hygiene or underlying health concerns. Swelling, drainage, or changes in feeding habits are all symptoms. Maintaining a clean workplace and responding quickly to any signs of illness can help prevent these illnesses.

6. Retention of Eggs:

Female Pancake Tortoises may develop egg retention, which causes them to be unable to lay eggs. This can result in drowsiness, edema, and discomfort. It is critical to provide adequate nesting locations and consult with a veterinarian if egg retention is anticipated.

SYMPTOMS OF Illness

1. Behavior Modifications:

Observing behavioral changes is critical in spotting potential health risks. Lethargy, a lack of interest in food, or changes in activity levels may indicate underlying issues. Any variations from their typical conduct should be investigated further.

2. Shell or skin abnormalities:

A Pancake Tortoise's shell and skin provide visual indications about its health. Softness, discolouration, or abnormalities in the shell could suggest a nutritional deficiency or a health problem. Changes in skin tone, such as paleness or darkening, can also indicate underlying issues.

3. Respiratory Problems:

Respiratory problems can be identified by audible breathing, wheezing, or nasal discharge. Tortoises may also breathe through their mouths, indicating respiratory difficulty. Any respiratory irregularities should be addressed as soon as possible because they can quickly worsen.

4. Swelling or Excessive Growth:

Swelling or abnormal growths on the torso, limbs, or head must be treated as away. These could be symptoms of infections, malignancies, or other underlying health problems. Physical examinations on a regular basis can help with early detection and action.

5. Eating Habit Changes:

A sudden loss of appetite or refusal to eat might be an early indicator of disease. It is critical to monitor eating habits and treat any changes as soon as possible in order to prevent nutritional deficits and related health problems.

6. Eye, nose, or mouth discharge:

Any discharge from the eyes, nose, or mouth should be taken seriously. It could be an indication of an infection or a respiratory problem. Inspection of these areas on a regular basis and obtaining veterinary assistance if discharge is noticed can help to prevent the progression of such illnesses.

7. Exceptional Fecal Characteristics:

Changes in fecal features, such as diarrhea, blood in the stool, or fecal shape anomalies, should be investigated. A veterinarian's regular fecal examinations aid in the detection and treatment of parasite infections and other gastrointestinal disorders.

PREVENTIVE MEASURES AND REGULAR CHECK-UPS

1. Veterinary Exams:

Regular veterinary examinations are required to keep Pancake Tortoises healthy. A skilled reptile veterinarian should perform thorough examinations, looking for symptoms of illness, deformities, and concerns. These examinations enable early detection and action.

2. Examinations of the feces:

Routine fecal exams are critical in the diagnosis and treatment of parasite diseases. Parasites can be present even if tortoises show no visible indications of sickness. Regular testing helps to ensure that any infestations are dealt with as soon as possible.

3. Dental examinations:

Dental health is important for reptiles, even though it is rarely emphasized. Pancake tortoises may suffer dental problems, particularly if their diet lacks the proper texture for natural wear. Regular dental exams help detect and manage potential issues.

4. Vaccinations:

Vaccinations against some diseases may benefit several reptiles, including Pancake Tortoises. Consult a reptile veterinarian to see if vaccines are necessary given the tortoise's life environment and potential exposure hazards.

5. Monitoring the Environment:

Monitor and maintain the environmental conditions within the enclosure on a regular basis. Ensure that the temperature, humidity, and illumination levels are appropriate for Pancake Tortoises. Consistent environmental conditions have a big impact on their overall health.

6. Hygiene Procedures:

In order to prevent illnesses, it is critical to establish proper hygiene practices. Clean the enclosure on a regular basis, eliminating any feces, uneaten food, or dirt. Make sure that the water dishes are cleaned and replenished with fresh water on a daily basis. Hygiene methods help to maintain a healthy and clean living environment.

7. Outreach Education:

Educating oneself about Pancake Tortoises' special needs and behaviors is a preventive practice in and of itself. Understanding their natural history, dietary needs, and prevalent health issues enables caregivers to provide the best care and discover any problems early.

CHAPTER 5

Socialization and Handling

The interaction between caregivers and Pancake Tortoises is a delicate ballet that demands patience, understanding, and respect for these unusual reptiles' natural habits. In this chapter, we will look at gentle handling techniques that promote a favorable interaction between people and tortoises, as well as the complexities of socializing several tortoises in order to create a happy living environment.

GENTLE MANAGEMENT TECHNIQUES

1. Personal Space is Respected:

Pancake Tortoises, like many other reptiles, cherish their privacy. When approaching the tortoise, approach it carefully and prevent unexpected movements. Allow the tortoise to adjust to your presence before making physical contact.

2. Lifting and Supporting:

Lifting a Pancake Tortoise requires sufficient body support to reduce stress. Scoop the turtle gently with both hands, making sure the entire body is supported. Excessive grabbing or squeezing of the shell is not recommended.

3. Prevent Prolonged Handling:

While Pancake Tortoises can endure brief handling sessions, prolonged interactions should be avoided. Respect their need for privacy and rest. Extensive handling sessions might induce tension, negatively impacting their well-being.

4. Body Language Interpretation:

Learn to decipher Pancake Tortoises' body language. Stress symptoms include withdrawing into a shell, hissing, or attempting to flee. Allow the tortoise to return to its enclosure and provide a calm environment if these indicators are present.

5. Interactions at the Ground Level:
When possible, allow for ground-level interactions. Allowing the tortoise to explore and move at its own pace on a safe, contained area encourages independence. This strategy corresponds to their semi-arboreal and ground-dwelling lifestyles.

6. Using Positive Reinforcement:
By providing treats or preferred meals, you might associate handling with happy experiences. This positive reinforcement fosters a link between handling and pleasant results, progressively increasing the tortoise's receptivity to interaction.

7. Approach Consistency:

When it comes to Pancake Tortoises, consistency is everything. Create a routine for approaching them and stick to it. Predictability fosters trust, and tortoises may become more at ease with handling over time.

8. Understand Individual Preferences:

Recognize that different tortoises have different tolerances for handling. Some people appreciate human interaction, while others prefer minimal contact. Knowing and respecting the preferences of each tortoise contributes to a positive handling experience.

9. Quiet and peaceful surroundings:

For handling sessions, choose a quiet and peaceful atmosphere. Pancake Tortoises can be stressed by loud noises, unexpected movements, or disruptions. A calm environment improves their comfort during encounters.

10. Hands should be washed before handling:

Before handling Pancake Tortoises, wash your hands to remove any smells or residues that may cause stress. Tortoises have a good sense of smell, thus keeping external aromas to a minimum aids in maintaining a calm connection.

NETWORKING WITH OTHER TORTOISES

1. Observation Time:

Gradually introduce fresh tortoises and begin with an observation period. Allow them to view and smell each other from afar before engaging in direct interaction. This earliest phase aids in the prevention of territorial disputes.

2. Size of Appropriate Enclosure:

Provide a large enough enclosure to comfortably house many tortoises. Space is essential for preventing overcrowding, territorial aggressiveness, and ensuring that each tortoise has access to the resources it need.

3. Several feeding and resting areas:

Include several feeding and basking spots within the enclosure. This lessens competition for resources and reduces the likelihood of conflict. Each turtle should have its own eating and basking area.

4. Social Dynamics Monitoring:

Observe the social dynamics of tortoises on a regular basis. While Pancake Tortoises are generally tolerant of their conspecifics, disagreements do develop on occasion. Keep an eye out for aggressive behavior, such as head bobbing, biting, or ramming, and intervene if required.

5. Gradually introducing tortoises:

Introduce new tortoises to an established group gradually. Use barriers first, allowing for visual interaction before making direct touch. Gradual introductions lessen stress and allow tortoises to become accustomed to each other's company.

6. Same-Sex Relationships:

If you have many Pancake Tortoises, consider same-sex pairings to reduce the possibility of reproductive conflicts. Males may exhibit territorial behavior, particularly during breeding season. Separating the sexes can assist to alleviate these problems.

7. Provide Hiding Places:

Include hiding places and shelters within the enclosure. Tortoises can find refuge in hiding spots when they are stressed or seeking seclusion. A well-balanced and stress-free environment is enhanced by enough hiding spots.

8. Look for Stress Indicators:

Stress can present itself in a variety of ways, such as changes in behavior, refusal to eat, or attempts to flee. Regularly monitor tortoises for indications of stress and handle any concerns that arise. Stress reduction is critical for their overall wellness.

9. New Additions Quarantine:

Consider a quarantine time when bringing a new tortoise to an existing group. This enables health assessments and the potential spread of diseases. Separate cages and close supervision should be included in quarantine.

10. Environmental Improvement:

Enhance the surroundings with a variety of features that encourage natural activities. A diversified and intriguing enclosure is made up of rocks, logs, and hiding places.

Environmental enrichment promotes mental stimulation and aids in the relief of potential boredom or tension.

CHAPTER 6

REPRODUCTION AND BREEDING

The exploration of Pancake Tortoise care includes the complicated processes of reproduction and breeding. In this chapter, we will delve into the intriguing world of Pancake Tortoise reproduction, decipher the complexities of nesting and incubation, and share ideas to help caretakers navigate the unique challenges and joys of Pancake Tortoise breeding.

BEING AWARE OF REPRODUCTIVE BEHAVIOR

1. Seasonal Effects:

Pancake tortoises, like many other reptiles, have seasonal reproductive habits that are controlled by environmental conditions. Breeding activity in their native habitats frequently coincides with the start of the rainy season, causing an increase in vegetation and good nesting conditions.

2. Male courting Rituals: Male Pancake Tortoises participate in courting rituals to attract females during the mating season. Head bobbing, circling, and gentle pushing may be used. As part of their courtship display, males may make low-frequency sounds. Recognizing breeding readiness requires an understanding of these actions.

3. Female Selection: Females choose mates based on a variety of variables, including their health and vigor during courtship. Female Pancake Tortoises may display receptive behaviors such as head nods or a relaxed posture to indicate their readiness to mate.

4. Copulation and Mating: In Pancake Tortoises, copulation occurs when the male mounts the female.

During the breeding season, the process may be repeated numerous times. Females keep sperm for an extended length of time after successful copulation, allowing them to lay several clutches of eggs without the requirement for immediate mating.

5. Egg Development and Laying: After successful copulation, females go through an egg development period. Pancake Tortoises normally lay small clutches of eggs, and egg-laying timing varies across individuals. As females prepare to lay eggs, nesting activities such as digging and looking for suitable places become visible.

Territorial Dynamics: Territorial dynamics in Pancake Tortoises influence breeding behavior. Males may form territories, and territorial or mating disputes may arise. When housing numerous tortoises or planning breeding endeavors, understanding these social dynamics is critical.

7. Gestation and Reproductive Cycles: Pancake Tortoises have a variable gestation period that ranges from 90 to 120 days. Temperature, day duration, and food availability all have an impact on reproductive cycles. To assist breeding, caregivers should notice these cycles and change environmental circumstances accordingly.

TIPS FOR NESTING AND INCUBATION 1. Nesting Site Selection: Providing appropriate nesting places is critical for successful reproduction. Nesting Pancake Tortoises prefer sandy or loamy soil. To facilitate digging, create dedicated nesting places within the enclosure with loose, well-draining dirt.

2. Monitoring Egg-Laying Behavior: Female Pancake Tortoises must be observed for indicators of nesting behavior. Restlessness, frequent digging, and investigation of prospective nesting locations are typical

characteristics. Caretakers should offer access to a suitable nesting habitat after these signals are identified.

3. Nesting cage Configuration: Create a separate nesting cage to provide a regulated environment for egg laying. This enclosure should be designed to imitate natural nesting conditions, with a substrate depth of at least 8 to 10 inches to allow for egg deposition.

4. Egg Collection and Handling: Collect deposited eggs with care to minimize little disturbance. Pancake Tortoise eggs are usually small and delicate. To avoid damage, handle them with extreme caution. Incubate the eggs in a wet incubation media, such as a vermiculite-water mixture.

5. Incubation Temperature and Humidity: To guarantee successful hatching, Pancake Tortoise eggs require precise incubation conditions. Keep the incubation

temperature between 86 and 89°F (30 and 32°C) and the relative humidity between 70 and 80%. These circumstances are designed to mimic the natural incubation environment.

6. Incubation Period: Pancake Tortoise eggs incubate for 90 to 120 days, depending on conditions such as temperature and humidity. Monitor the incubation environment on a regular basis and make adjustments as needed to maximize conditions for growing embryos.

7. Candling for Viability: Candling, which involves shining a light through an egg, allows caregivers to check the viability of growing embryos. Non-viable eggs may be discolored, lack vascularization, or exhibit other defects. To avoid problems, remove any non-viable eggs as soon as possible.

8. Post-Hatching Care: Once the eggs hatch, give a separate enclosure with acceptable environmental conditions for the hatchlings. Provide a shallow water dish for drinking and a calcium-rich feed appropriate for their size.

9. Keep careful records of the breeding process, including copulation dates, egg-laying dates, and incubation conditions. Keeping thorough records aids caregivers in recognizing patterns, adjusting breeding circumstances, and dealing with any problems that may occur.

10. Hatchling Health examinations: Perform thorough health examinations on hatchlings. Keep an eye on their development, behavior, and feeding patterns. Address any signs of illness as soon as possible, and seek advice from a reptile veterinarian on how to care for young Pancake Tortoises.

Breeding Pancake Tortoises is a rewarding but difficult effort that necessitates a thorough grasp of their natural behaviors and requirements. Caretakers can contribute to the conservation of the species and share in the thrill of witnessing the growth and development of future generations by observing and respecting the reproductive dynamics of these rare reptiles. The following chapters will delve into legal issues, troubleshooting tips, and advanced care methods, providing a thorough introduction to proper Pancake Tortoise ownership.

CHAPTER 7

LEGAL CONCERNS

The legal environment that governs the possession and administration of these intriguing reptiles is explored in order to ensure proper care and ownership of Pancake Tortoises. In this chapter, we will look at the essential legal concerns for responsible Pancake Tortoise ownership, emphasizing compliance with wildlife rules, the acquisition of licenses, and the significance of thorough documentation.

OBEDIENCE TO WILDLIFE REGULATIONS

1. Regulations for Specific Species:

Pancake Tortoises (Malacochersus tornieri) are subject to a variety of wildlife legislation and conservation laws. Caretakers must get acquainted with species-specific rules that may apply at the municipal, national, and international levels before purchasing a Pancake Tortoise.

2. Protected Status: Due to their vulnerability in the wild, Pancake Tortoises are frequently subject to wildlife conservation regulations. This protected classification is intended to reduce unlawful trafficking, boost

conservation activities, and assure responsible ownership.

3. Investigate Local Legislation: Wildlife rules vary greatly between places. Caretakers should properly examine and comprehend the local regulations regarding the possession, trade, and breeding of Pancake Tortoises. Local wildlife authorities or government wildlife management bodies can provide useful information.

4. Appendix II of the Convention on International Trade in Endangered Species of Wild Fauna and Flora (CITES) lists Pancake Tortoises. This designation restricts international trade and emphasizes the importance of obtaining permissions when crossing borders with Pancake Tortoises.

5. Ethical Purchasing: Responsible Pancake Tortoise ownership begins with acquiring individuals in an ethical manner. It is critical to confirm that any tortoises in your possession were obtained legally and ethically, in accordance with conservation principles and rules.

6. Trade limitations: Some governments place trade limitations on Pancake Tortoises, making it illegal to buy, sell, or trade these reptiles without a permit. Understanding and abiding to these rules is critical to avoiding legal ramifications.

7. Avoiding Illicit trading: The illegal trading of Pancake Tortoises endangers their wild populations. Caretakers must deliberately refrain from engaging in or supporting unlawful trading activity. Purchasing tortoises from trustworthy breeders or approved sources aids in the fight against the illegal pet trade.

8. Record-Keeping for Traceability: It is critical to keep detailed records of Pancake Tortoises' procurement and ownership history. This paperwork facilitates tracking and proves adherence to legal and ethical standards. Records should include information such as the place of origin, the date of purchase, and any permissions acquired.

DOCUMENTS AND PERMITS

1. Permit Requirements: Permits are required in many areas for the possession, breeding, and trade of Pancake Tortoises. Before obtaining or indulging in any activities with these reptiles, caretakers must identify and secure the necessary licenses. Wildlife authorities or associated government bodies often issue permits.

2. Application Procedures: The procedure for getting permissions differs by location. The application procedures, relevant papers, and any associated fees

should be clearly understood by caregivers. It is best to start the permit application process well in advance of purchasing Pancake Tortoises.

3. Species Registration: Caretakers may be required to register their Pancake Tortoises with local wildlife authorities in some situations. Registration allows authorities to monitor the captive population and assures that owners are responsible for their tortoises' well-being and legal status.

4. Transport Permits: Transporting Pancake Tortoises across borders or within specific regions frequently necessitates the acquisition of additional permits. These licenses are required for legal movement and must be secured prior to beginning any travel with the tortoises.

5. CITES Permits for International Trade: The international trade of Pancake Tortoises is governed by

CITES. To maintain compliance with international regulations, caregivers who engage in cross-border transactions, including as buying from or selling to individuals in other countries, must get CITES permits.

6. Health Certificates: When transporting Pancake Tortoises, health certificates may be necessary. These certificates verify the tortoises' health and may be required for crossing borders or participating in particular events, such as exhibitions or shows.

7. Breeding Program Documentation: If involved in Pancake Tortoise breeding initiatives, caretakers should keep complete records of breeding activities. This includes information on pairings, egg-laying, incubation, and hatchlings. Documentation is extensive, demonstrating responsible breeding procedures.

8. Veterinary Certifications: Some jurisdictions may demand veterinary certifications to accompany permit applications. These certifications normally attest to the Pancake Tortoises' health status and may include specifics like disease testing and general health assessments.

9. Permit Renewal and Compliance Checks: Permits frequently have expiration dates, and caretakers must be attentive in renewing them as needed. Furthermore, wildlife authorities may undertake compliance checks to ensure that permit holders follow legal and ethical guidelines.

10. Educational and Conservation permissions: Caretakers may seek permissions for educational or conservation reasons under specified circumstances. Specific activities, such as educational presentations or participation in conservation campaigns, may be

permitted under these permissions. In their permit applications, caregivers should clearly state the objective of such activities.

The legal environment of Pancake Tortoise ownership necessitates adherence to compliance, ethical procedures, and conservation principles. Caretakers contribute to the conservation of Pancake Tortoises and demonstrate responsible ownership by getting the proper licenses, complying to wildlife regulations, and maintaining rigorous paperwork. The following chapters will go into troubleshooting guidelines, advanced care methods, and community engagement, giving a comprehensive handbook for individuals concerned about the well-being and conservation of these amazing reptiles.

CHAPTER 8

Troubleshooting Manual

Owning and caring for Pancake Tortoises has its rewards and drawbacks. This troubleshooting guide is intended to aid caregivers in detecting and managing troublesome behaviors, as well as to provide rapid answers to frequent problems. Understanding and resolving difficulties ranging from behavioral concerns to health-related issues is critical for the well-being of Pancake Tortoises.

BEHAVIORAL ISSUES

1. Lethargy:

Problem: A sluggish Pancake Tortoise could indicate a number of underlying difficulties, such as health concerns, poor environmental circumstances, or stress.

CAUSES AND SOLUTIONS POSSIBLE:

Examine the tortoise's health to ensure it is in good health. A comprehensive inspection should be performed by a reptile veterinarian.

Optimal Environment: Examine and optimize the temperature, lighting, and humidity levels in the enclosure. Pancake tortoises require precise environmental conditions to survive, and variations can have an impact on their activity levels.

2. Refusal to Consume:

Problem: Loss of appetite can be caused by health problems, dietary concerns, or stress.

CAUSES AND SOLUTIONS POSSIBLE:

Health Examination: Perform a physical examination to rule out any underlying illnesses or parasites.

Dietary Assessment: Examine the diet to verify it is well-balanced and suitable for Pancake Tortoises. Provide a selection of fresh, high-quality greens and veggies.

Temperature and illumination: Make sure the enclosure has the appropriate temperature and UVB illumination, as these aspects influence appetite and digestion.

3. Aggression Against Conspecifics

Problem: Pancake Tortoises may exhibit aggressive behavior, particularly during breeding season or during territorial disputes.

CAUSES AND SOLUTIONS POSSIBLE

Separation: If you have more than one tortoise, try establishing different cages or dividing the current space to reduce territorial conflicts.

Same-Sex Pairing: Use same-sex pairings to lessen mate rivalry and territorial aggressiveness.

Enrich the enclosure with hiding places, multiple feeding areas, and enrichment factors to lessen stress and hostility.

4. Abnormalities in the Shell:

Problem: Shell abnormalities, such as pyramiding or softening, can occur as a result of poor feeding, a lack of UVB exposure, or insufficient enclosure conditions.

CAUSES AND SOLUTIONS POSSIBLE:

Dietary Changes: To assist appropriate shell formation, have a well-balanced, calcium-rich diet.

UVB Exposure: Make UVB lighting available to aid calcium absorption and shell health.

Review and alter the cage configuration to ensure that it suits the specific needs of Pancake Tortoises, including appropriate substrate and hiding locations.

5. Respiratory Problems:

Wheezing, hard breathing, or nasal discharge can all suggest respiratory problems, which are frequently caused by inappropriate temperature or humidity levels.

Causes and possible solutions:

Environmental Assessment: Evaluate and regulate the temperature and humidity of the enclosure to meet the needs of Pancake Tortoises.

Ventilation: Maintain adequate ventilation in the enclosure to avoid respiratory difficulties.

Consultation with a veterinarian: If respiratory symptoms persist, seek immediate medical attention because they might develop to significant health problems.

QUICK SOLUTIONS FOR COMMON PROBLEMS

1. Overheating:

Problem: If exposed to too high temperatures, Pancake Tortoises can overheat.

SOLUTIONS IN ADVANCE:

Temperature Control: Lower the enclosure's ambient temperature by changing heating elements or providing shade.

Cooling Zones: Designate cool zones within the cage so that the tortoises can regulate their body temperature.

2. Dehydration:

Problem: Dehydration can arise owing to a lack of water or a lack of moisture in the diet.

SOLUTIONS IN ADVANCE:

Hydration Stations: Provide tortoises with shallow water dishes for drinking.

Moisture-rich foods, such as leafy greens, should be included in the diet to help with hydration.

3. Infections caused by parasites:

Internal or external parasites can cause health problems in Pancake Tortoises.

SOLUTIONS IN ADVANCE:

Fecal Examination: Perform fecal examinations on a regular basis to diagnose and treat parasite illnesses.

Hygiene Practices: Keep your enclosure clean to reduce the possibility of parasite infections.

4. Female Egg Retention:

Female Pancake Tortoises may have trouble producing eggs, causing discomfort.

SOLUTIONS IN ADVANCE:

Nesting places: Provide suitable nesting places with sufficient substrate for egg laying.

Veterinary Care: If egg retention is suspected, seek immediate veterinary care to avoid complications.

5. Handling Anxiety:

Overhandling causes stress in Pancake Tortoises, affecting their behavior and health.

SOLUTIONS IN ADVANCE:

Reduce Handling Frequency: To reduce stress, limit handling sessions.

Gentle Approach: When handling is required, use gentle techniques and avoid abrupt movements.

6. Insufficient UVB exposure:

Problem: Inadequate UVB exposure might lead to calcium shortages and shell difficulties.

SOLUTIONS IN ADVANCE:

UVB Lighting: Make sure the enclosure has adequate UVB lighting to facilitate calcium absorption.

outside Exposure: Provide outside access to natural sunshine, which contains beneficial UVB rays, whenever possible.

7. Environmental Improvement:

Boredom or a lack of excitement can contribute to behavioral problems.

SOLUTIONS IN ADVANCE:

Introduce varied materials like as rocks, logs, and hiding locations to foster natural behaviors.

Rotate décor: To keep the atmosphere interesting, rotate the layout of décor and hiding areas on a regular basis.

8. Dietary Variation:

Problem: A lack of dietary variety can lead to nutritional deficits.

SOLUTIONS IN ADVANCE:

Diverse Diet: Provide a variety of greens, vegetables, and fruits to provide a well-rounded diet.

Consider calcium and vitamin supplements as needed, particularly for growing tortoises.

9. Territorial Conflicts:

Problem: Aggressive behavior among tortoises living in the same enclosure.

SOLUTIONS IN ADVANCE:

Separation:* Separate aggressive tortoises for the time being.

Environmental Changes: Rearrange the enclosure layout to accommodate more hiding locations and eating sites.

10. Monitoring on a regular basis:

Problem: A lack of consistent monitoring can cause issues to be detected later.

SOLUTIONS IN ADVANCE:

Observations on a daily basis: Conduct daily observations to check behavior, appetite, and overall well-being.

Keep a diary of your observations and any changes in behavior or health.

BONUS CHAPTER

FAQS

1.Q: How long does a Pancake Tortoise live on average?

A: With proper care, Pancake Tortoises can survive in captivity for 25 to 30 years.

2. Q: How large can Pancake Tortoises grow?

A: Adult Pancake Tortoises can grow to be 6 to 7 inches (15 to 18 cm) long.

3. Q: What kind of food should I give my Pancake Tortoise?

A varied diet of leafy greens, vegetables, and occasional fruits is recommended for Pancake Tortoises.

4. Q: Is UVB illumination required for Pancake Tortoises?

A: Yes, UVB lighting is essential for Pancake Tortoises' calcium absorption and shell health.

5. Q: How often should I clean the enclosure of my Pancake Tortoise?

A: Daily spot cleaning is recommended, with a comprehensive enclosure cleaning at least once a month.

6. Can Pancake Tortoises be kept together?

A: Pancake Tortoises can be housed together, but sufficient space and social dynamics must be observed to avoid aggression.

7. Q: Which substrate is suitable for a Pancake Tortoise enclosure?

A: As a substrate, a mixture of coconut coir and cypress mulch works well, offering an appropriate texture for digging.

8. Q: How can I tell if my Pancake Tortoise is ill?

A: Changes in behavior, appetite, or appearance are all symptoms of disease. If you find any irregularities, consult a veterinarian.

9. Q: Do Pancake Tortoises sleep?

A: Hibernation is not required in captivity, however they may endure a period of reduced activity in cooler temperatures.

10. Q: Do Pancake Tortoises have the ability to swim?

A: Pancake Tortoises are not strong swimmers and should avoid deep water. Make shallow water available for drinking and soaking.

11. Q: How can I make a hiding place in the enclosure?

A: Create safe hiding places for Pancake Tortoises using rocks, logs, or commercial hides.

12. Q: Are Pancake Tortoises suitable for novices?

A: While Pancake Tortoises are not the simplest turtle to care for, they are manageable for novices with adequate research and devotion.

13. Q: Can I keep Pancake Tortoises outside in an enclosure?

A: Outdoor enclosures can be used, but they must be protected from harsh temperatures and predators.

14. Q: What temperature range is best for a Pancake Tortoise enclosure?

A: Daytime temperatures should be between 80 and 90 degrees Fahrenheit (27 and 32 degrees Celsius), with a little dip at night.

15. How frequently do Pancake Tortoises lay eggs?

A: Female Pancake Tortoises normally lay eggs once or twice a year, in the spring or summer.

16. Q: Can I feed commercial tortoise pellets to my Pancake Tortoise?

A: While commercial pellets can be included in the diet, they should not be the primary source of nutrition. A diversified, natural diet is required.

17. Q: What are the basking places in the enclosure for?

A: Basking places give a warm environment for Pancake Tortoises to maintain their body temperature and aid in digestion.

18. Q: What should I do with a Pancake Tortoise?

A: Handle them gently, correctly support the body, and be aware of their desire for personal space.

19. Q: Do Pancake Tortoises know who their owners are?

A: While Pancake Tortoises are not as gregarious as other pets, they can become used to their owners and may exhibit recognition.

20. Q: Is it possible to breed Pancake Tortoises at home?
A: Careful thought must be given to aspects like as health, genetics, and legal requirements while breeding. Seek advice before attempting to breed.

21. Q: Can Pancake Tortoises communicate?
A: Pancake Tortoises may generate low-frequency sounds during courting or in distress.

22. Q: Do Pancake Tortoises come in different colors?
A: Pancake tortoises are typically brown to tan in color with dark markings, though variances within this range are normal.

23. Q: Do Pancake Tortoises get along with other reptiles?

A: reduce cohabitation with other reptiles to reduce stress and probable conflicts.

24. Q: What does the Pancake Tortoise's flattened shell mean?

A: Their flattened shell helps them wedge into rocky crevices for protection.

25. Q: Do Pancake Tortoises require any special vaccinations?

A: Pancake Tortoises are not normally vaccinated, although frequent health checkups are required.

26. Q: How can I keep Pancake Tortoises' beaks from becoming overgrown?

A: Provide a variety of chewing items and, if necessary, see a veterinarian for beak trimming.

27. Q: Can Pancake Tortoises be trained to use the toilet?

A: While they cannot be trained in the usual sense, they do defecate in specific regions, making spot cleaning easier.

28. Q: Can I put fake plants in the enclosure?

A: Yes, but make sure they're non-toxic and well-anchored to avoid consumption or harm.

29. Q: Do Pancake Tortoises require any special grooming?

A: Grooming requirements are modest; provide them with a water dish for soaking, which aids in shedding.

30. Q: How do I have sex with Pancake Tortoises?

A: It can be difficult to tell, but males typically have a concave plastron, whilst females may have a flatter or slightly convex plastron.

31. Q: Can you keep Pancake Tortoises in groups?

A: Yes, but keep an eye out for territorial behaviors and make sure each tortoise has enough room and resources.

32. Q: How can I make a nesting space in the enclosure?

A: Provide a sandy ground with at least 8-10 inches of depth to allow for digging and nesting.

33. Q: Do Pancake Tortoises need a water dish to drink from?

A: Yes, a small water dish should be provided for drinking, soaking, and keeping proper hydration.

34. Q: Can I train Pancake Tortoises to eat from my hand?

A: Some Pancake Tortoises may learn to associate feeding with your presence with patience and positive reinforcement.

35. Q: Can Pancake Tortoises be kept as pets?

A: Check your local wildlife rules; licenses may be required in some regions to legally keep Pancake Tortoises.

36. Q: How do I keep Pancake Tortoises from getting respiratory infections?

A: Maintain proper temperature and humidity levels in the cage, as well as proper ventilation.

37. Q: Do Pancake Tortoises have the ability to climb?

A: They may attempt to climb low objects while not being expert climbers. Ascertain that the enclosure is escape-proof.

38. Q: What woods are suitable for Pancake Tortoise enclosures?

A: Avoid using toxic woods; instead, use cypress, oak, and non-resinous woods.

39. Q: Can you keep Pancake Tortoises in a glass enclosure?

A: Glass enclosures can be utilized, but they must be monitored for overheating and well ventilated.

40. Do Pancake Tortoises need supplements?

A: Calcium and vitamin supplements may be required depending on food and environmental factors. Consult a veterinarian.

41. Q: Are there any special precautions to take during the winter?

A: In captivity, Pancake Tortoises may exhibit lower activity in cooler temps; provide them with a warm hideaway.

42. Q: Can Pancake Tortoises be microchipped in order to be identified?

A: Microchipping for identifying purposes is conceivable, though less popular than in some pets.

43. Q: Do Pancake Tortoises enjoy sunbathing in the wild?
A: They do ask to regulate their body temperature, which should be reproduced in captivity.

44. Q: Is it possible to litter train Pancake Tortoises?
A: While they cannot be trained like certain mammals, they frequently defecate in specific locations of the enclosure.

45. Q: What rocks are suitable for Pancake Tortoise enclosures?
A: Smooth, non-toxic rocks can be used, but sharp edges should be avoided to avoid harm.

46. Q: How do I keep female Pancake Tortoises from laying eggs?

A: Provide appropriate nesting opportunities, and seek veterinarian treatment as soon as possible if problems emerge.

47. Q: Can Pancake Tortoises coexist with other tortoises?

A: To avoid stress and potential conflicts, it is typically advised to avoid living with different tortoise species.

48. Q: Can Pancake Tortoises be housed in a bioactive environment?

A: Yes, bioactive environments containing live plants and healthy microbes can improve the tortoise's surroundings.

49. Q: How can I teach male Pancake Tortoises not to be aggressive?

A: Provide enough space, add hiding places, and consider separate enclosures during mating season.

50. Q: Can Pancake Tortoises be kept indoors all year?

A: Yes, but make sure they have adequate warmth, lighting, and humidity levels to mimic their native environment.

www.ingramcontent.com/pod-product-compliance
Lightning Source LLC
Chambersburg PA
CBHW060956260726

48661CB00005B/1895